D1458610

Traditional Crafts from

AFRICA

Traditional Crafts from
AFRICA

by Florence Temko

with illustrations by Randall Gooch
and photographs by Robert L. and Diane Wolfe

Lerner Publications Company • Minneapolis

To Bob, Joan, Yolanda, and Tyler

Over the years, I have tucked away bits of information in my files
that have contributed to my fascination with crafts. They were
gathered mainly from personal meetings, books, magazines,
libraries, and museums. I regret it is no longer possible to
disentangle these many and varied resources, but I would like
to acknowledge gratefully and humbly everyone who has helped
to make this book possible.
—Florence Temko

Library of Congress Cataloging-in-Publication Data

Temko, Florence.
   Traditional crafts from Africa / by Florence Temko.
     p. cm.—(Culture crafts)
   Includes bibliographical references and index.
   ISBN 0-8225-2936-X
   1. Handicraft—Africa—Juvenile literature. [1. Handicraft—Africa.] I. Title. II.
Series.
T T115.T46 1996
745'.096—dc20   95-8109

Manufactured in the United States of America
1 2 3 4 5 6 – JR – 01 00 99 98 97 96

CONTENTS

WHAT ARE CRAFTS?

All over the world, people need baskets, bowls, clothes, and tools. People now make many of these things in factories. But long ago, people made what they needed by hand. They formed clay and metal pots for cooking. They wove cloth to wear. They made baskets to carry food. We call these things "crafts" when they are made by hand.

Grandparents and parents taught children how to make crafts. While they worked, the elders told stories. These stories told of their family's culture—all of the ideas and customs that a group of people believe in and practice. Children learned these stories as they learned the ways of making crafts. They painted or carved symbols from those stories on their crafts.

Year after year, methods and symbols were passed from parents to children. Still, each bowl or basket they made would look a little different. A craft made by hand—even by the same person—never turns out the exact same way twice.

People who are very good at making crafts are called artisans. Many artisans still use the old methods. They make useful things for themselves and their homes. Today, some artisans also sell their crafts to earn money.

Left to right: A painted tile from Turkey, a Pueblo Indian pitcher, a pot from Peru, and a porcelain dish from China

MATERIALS AND SUPPLIES

Some of the suggested materials for the crafts in this book are the same as those used by African artisans. Others will give you almost the same results. Most materials can be found at home or purchased at local stores. Check your telephone book for art material, crafts, and teacher supply stores in your area. Whenever you can, try to use recyclable materials—and remember to reuse or recycle the scraps from your projects.

MEASUREMENTS

Sizes are given in inches. If you prefer to use the metric system, you can use the conversion chart on page 58. Because fractions can be hard to work with, round all metric measurements to the nearest whole number.

FINISHES

The crafts in this book that are made from paper will last longer if you brush or sponge them with a thin coat of finish. These are some choices:

White glue (Elmer's or another brand) is the most widely available. Use it at full strength or dilute it with a few drops of water. Apply it with a brush or small sponge. (The sponge should be thrown away after you use it.) White glue dries clear.

Acrylic medium is sold in art supply stores. It handles much like white glue. You can choose a glossy (shiny) finish or a matte (dull) finish.

AFRICAN CRAFTS

The vast continent of Africa lies between the Atlantic Ocean to the west and the Indian Ocean to the east. The Mediterranean Sea lies to the north. Africa has mountain ranges, deserts, tropical rain forests, coastal swamps, and grassy plains. Each area contains a wide variety of trees and plants, minerals, and other natural resources. Crafts produced in different areas of Africa are influenced by the materials found in each region.

The Sahara Desert stretches across North Africa, forming a natural barrier to the rest of Africa. Artistic styles in North Africa are very different from those below the Sahara. In northeastern Africa, the ancient Egyptians used desert sand to create glass sculptures and jewelry as long ago as 3,000 B.C. The art of making paper from papyrus plants also originated in Egypt, where papyrus grows along the Nile River.

Both west and central Africans have a rich tradition of carving masks and figures from the trees of the tropical rain forests. These masks are often carved from a single piece of wood and decorated with paint. The Asante, the Bambara, and the Dogon peoples each have their own styles of woodcarving.

In East Africa, carvings are made from a soft stone called soapstone, as well as from wood. The Makonde people carve masks from the dense black wood of ebony trees, which are found in the tropical forests of southeastern Africa.

Some Africans make jewelry from shells, nuts, and stones. When Europeans arrived in southern Africa more than 400 years ago, they traded glass beads with the African people. The Ndbele people now make colorful beaded jewelry. The Ndbele are also known for the brightly colored geometric designs they paint on the insides and outsides of their houses.

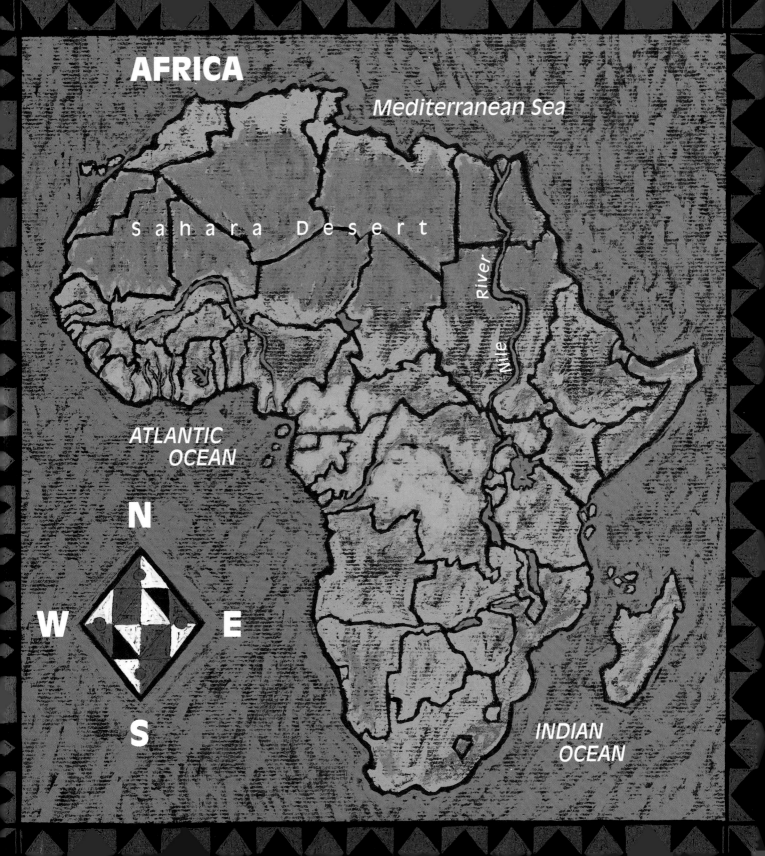

Senufo Mud Painting

With a mixture of mud and paint, you can create striking Senufo designs. Try them on T-shirts and handmade greeting cards.

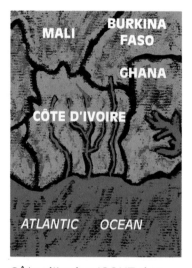

MUD PAINTING

A group of people called the Senufo (seh-NOO-foh) live in the northern part of Côte d'Ivoire. Senufo artisans use dark, slushy river mud to paint fabric. Sometimes this fabric is made into clothing. Hunters wear clothes with mud paintings of animals. They believe the spirits of these animals will protect them from danger and bring a successful

Côte d'Ivoire (COHT dee-VWAHR) means "Ivory Coast" in French. Côte d'Ivoire lies on the west coast of Africa. Its three long rivers flow south to the Atlantic Ocean. The river soil makes a rich, dark mud that stains cloth just like paint.

hunt. The black-and-white designs blend with shadows and camouflage the hunters.

TECHNIQUE

Senufo people weave fabric in narrow strips. They sew several strips together to make clothing. They stretch and nail the fabric to a wooden board. Then the fabric is ready to decorate with mud paint.

First, the Senufo artisans collect mud from nearby swamps. This mud makes a deep black paint. Then they draw outlines of animals and other designs with a knife blade dipped in dye. The thin liquid dye is made from boiled leaves. When the outline has dried, they use the knife blade or a toothbrush to fill in parts with the heavier mud paint. Sometimes children learn this way of painting by filling in their parents' outlines for them.

Mud painters often draw crocodiles, turtles, monkeys, and lizards known as chameleons (kuh-MEE-lee-uhns).

These animals are common to Côte d'Ivoire.

According to Senufo legends, they were the first animals created on the earth.

Senufo artisans use mud paint to make pictures of hunters and animals. The Senufo paint on cloth that they weave themselves.

HOW-TO PROJECT

Try the Senufo way of painting cloth yourself. The mud near your home may not stain the way African mud does. But if you mix in a little paint, any kind of dirt will work just as well.

Before you start, take a look at the examples of Senufo mud paintings shown on pages 12 and 13. The artisan works with only one color of mud. Sometimes the artisan fills in a whole area with mud paint. Different shades are shown by painting dots, stripes, and crossed lines.

You will fill in outlines just like you would in a coloring book. But in this case, the outlines are not ready-made. You create them yourself. Before you start, think about what you want to paint. You may want to make a rough sketch on paper first.

Caution: Handle permanent ink and paint carefully. Toothbrushes can spatter paint, and any marks on your clothes will not wash out!

You need:

½ cup dirt
½ cup nontoxic acrylic or poster paint (blue or black will look most like authentic Senufo mud paint)
T-shirt or unbleached muslin
Wide felt-tip pens, black, permanent type
Quart-sized disposable container
Piece of wire screen or kitchen strainer (big enough to fit over mouth of container)
Toothbrush
Small paintbrush
Several newspapers

1 Put dirt on a wire screen or strainer and set it on top of a disposable container. Slowly run water over the dirt and let the mud run through the screen into the container. Once all the dirt has been strained this way, let the container sit until the mud sinks to the bottom. You may want to let the container sit overnight.

2 Pour off the extra water. Mix the paint into the mud.

3 Cover your work area with newspapers. If you are painting a shirt, place a layer of newspaper between the front and back of the shirt. Smooth the shirt flat.

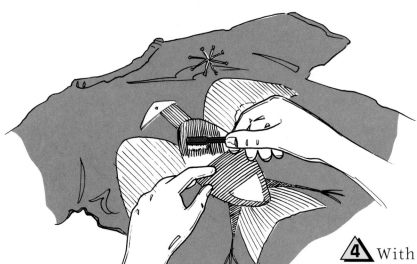

4 With the black felt-tip pen, draw your picture or design on the fabric. With a toothbrush, fill in the large areas with the mud paint. You can paint patterns of lines or dots by dipping a small paintbrush in the mud paint.

5 Let the painting dry. Hand wash the shirt in cool water and hang to dry before wearing.

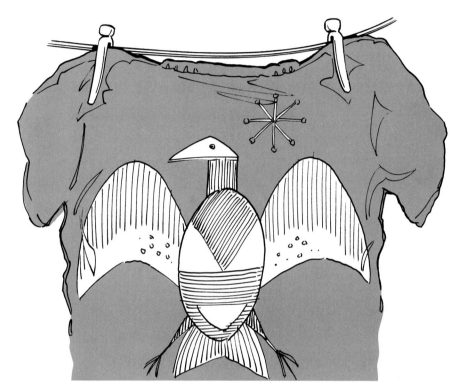

WHAT ELSE YOU CAN DO

Other Clothing: You can use the same techniques to paint vests, skirts, scarves—anything made of plain cloth. Remember to place newspaper between the front and back of the garment so that the ink does not run through to the wrong side.

Painting on Paper: If you don't want to wear your creation, make small, painted fabric pictures instead. Glue them to construction paper for greeting cards or place mats.

Asante Adinkra Stamping

Colorful adinkra patterns decorate place mats and napkins. Try using different colors of ink on both cloth and paper.

ADINKRA STAMPING

The Asante (ah-SAHN-teh) people live in western Africa. They do a special type of printing on fabric called adinkra (ah-DINK-rah) stamping. They decorate fabric with geometric shapes, such as crosses, spirals, and zigzags. Patterns are created by printing repeated rows of shapes with a stamping tool. The Asante make these fabrics into clothes.

Once, adinkra clothing was worn only for funerals. (Adinkra means "good-bye.") Now adinkra stamps adorn everyday clothes, as well as curtains and pillows.

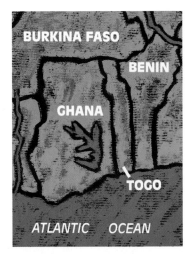

The country of Ghana (GAH-nah) has a forest area known as the Asante region, where hard-skinned gourds called calabashes grow. The Asante people dry and carve calabashes to use as bowls, ladles, and stamps to decorate cloth.

TECHNIQUE

To make adinkra cloth, artisans put dye on patterned blocks that are cut from dried calabashes. The dye is made from boiled tree bark. Iron ore makes the dye black. Egg whites are added for a high gloss.

Adinkra designs are stamped inside squares drawn on fabric. The squares are formed by lines that are drawn up and down, then across the fabric. By dipping a wooden comb into the thin dye, Asante artisans can draw several even lines at once. Each square is stamped with one pattern that is repeated several times.

Spiderweb:
WISDOM, CREATIVITY

The shapes on adinkra cloth have special meanings that give information about the wearer.

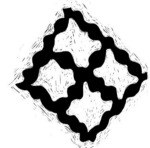

Fence:
SECURITY, LOVE

For example, a double circle with spokes on either the inside or the outside, called a hene (HEH-nay), is a symbol worn by a royal person.

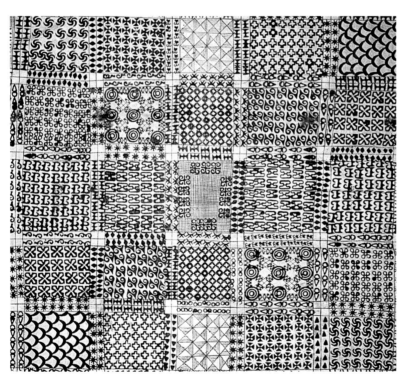

Asante artisans made this adinkra cloth more than 100 years ago.

PATIENCE

HOW-TO PROJECT ▮▮▮▮▮▮▮▮

Adinkra stamping is a fun and easy way to make vivid patterns. Instead of a calabash, which takes a long time to dry and prepare, your stamping tool can be a slice of firm potato. Potatoes print well on paper.

Caution: Ask an adult to help you cut the stamp pattern into the potato. Also, handle stamp pads and ink carefully. Any marks on your clothes will not wash out.

You need:

2 or 3 firm potatoes
Stamp pad
Stamp pad ink (for reinking)
Permanent felt-tip pen
Ruler
Several pieces of plain white
   paper
Table knife or plastic knife
Several paper towels
Several newspapers

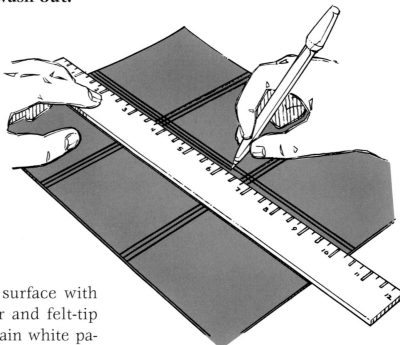

1 Cover your work surface with newspaper. Use a ruler and felt-tip pen to draw lines on plain white paper. Follow the sample shown to draw lines up and down, then across the paper to form squares. (They don't have to be perfect.)

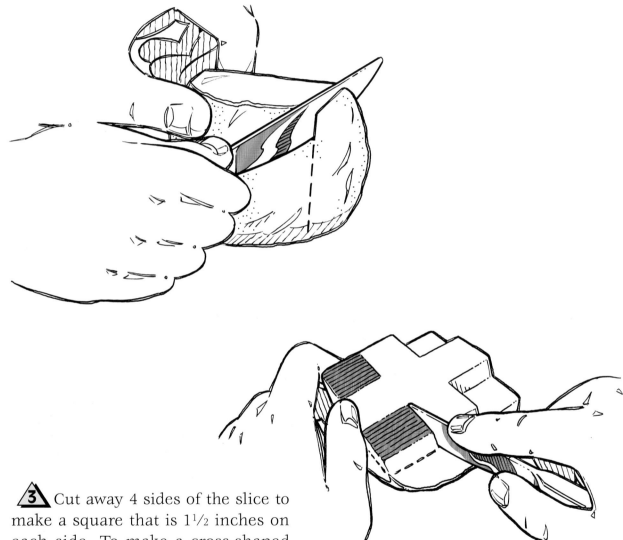

2 Prepare your stamp. Cut a slice of potato about ¾ inch thick with a table knife.

3 Cut away 4 sides of the slice to make a square that is 1½ inches on each side. To make a cross-shaped stamp, cut away a smaller square in each of the slice's 4 corners. You'll be cutting away the shaded areas shown in the diagram.

4 Before you begin to print, dry the potato stamp with a paper towel. Press the stamp on a well-inked stamp pad. (If the pad becomes dry, reink the pad with extra ink.)

5 Stamp the pattern in rows inside one of the squares on the paper. Cut more potato stamps in other shapes for printing inside the other squares. In the sample shown, you can see the stamps are used in more than one square, but in different ways. The same cross was stamped on the diagonal in square 1 and straight up and down in square 5. In square 3, two different shapes have been combined.

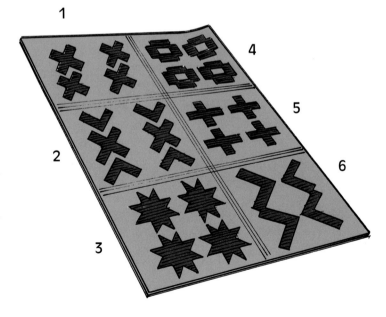

WHAT ELSE YOU CAN DO

Greeting Cards: Fold an 8½- by 11-inch piece of paper in half. Print adinkra patterns on the front.

Adinkra T-shirts: You can stamp adinkra patterns on T-shirts with acrylic or fabric paints. Use a small piece of foam sponge to apply the paint to the potato stamp. Throw away the sponge after use. (Always wash out any spatters of paint at once. Otherwise they will dry and you won't be able to remove them.)

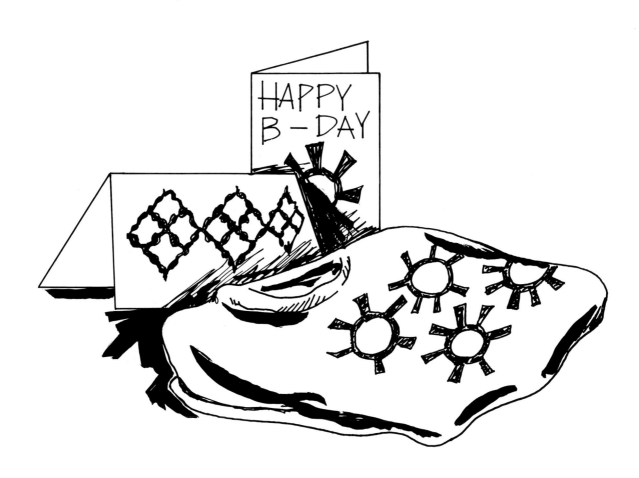

Fon Story Pictures

Story pictures use bright pieces of felt or construction paper.

STORY PICTURES

The Fon people of Benin tell their legends with brightly colored cloth pictures. At one time, Benin was known as Dahomey (dah-HOH-mee), and it was one of the most powerful kingdoms in West Africa. To show off their wealth and teach people about their history, Dahomey kings asked artists to make colorful story banners and umbrellas. Dahomey banners would hang behind the king's throne and

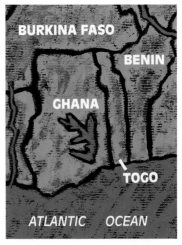

The Fon people of Benin (beh-NEEN) live in the southern part of the country and work as farmers. Their artwork shows the many kinds of animals found in Benin—buffalo, wild hogs, herons, egrets, lions, and fish.

the umbrella would shade him during royal ceremonies. The kingdom of Dahomey lost its power and wealth long ago. The chiefs of the Fon people still use the banners for special ceremonies, but the story cloths are no longer made strictly for kings. They can be found in many Benin homes. Tourists can buy beautiful story cloths in African markets.

TECHNIQUE

Story pictures are made with cotton cloth. The figures are cut from separate cloths of red, blue, white, and other strong colors. They are sewn to a background that is usually black. This method of sewing is called appliqué (ap-lih-KAY).

Story pictures tell of great battles or other important events using cutouts of people, ships, and animals.

Pictures of kings are often surrounded by drums, lions, or leopards.

Since one Dahomey legend says that lightning never strikes a pineapple, Dahomey kings often used the pineapple as a symbol on their banners.

These men sew story pictures in Abomey, Benin.

HOW-TO PROJECT

You can make your own story pictures with felt, construction paper, or other art paper. Before you glue the pieces to your background, move them around until you like your design. (Hint: Using a removable glue stick lets you move your pictures around to change the story as you go.)

You need:

Several pieces of felt (sometimes this comes with adhesive backing, so you don't need glue) or construction paper in black and bright colors
Felt-tip marker
White glue or glue stick
Scissors
Pencil

1 With a marker, draw the characters from the story that you want to tell onto pieces of felt. Design your picture with figures that are important to you. If you love baseball, show a player, a hat, and a bat. Tell a story from your life.

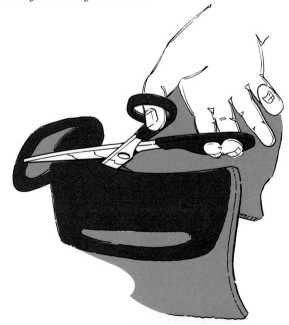

2 Cut the figures from the felt. Use leftover scraps in contrasting colors for eyes, mouths, and other features.

3 Glue the cutout figures to a large piece of black felt. Cut 4 long strips of a different color felt and glue them around the sides of your story picture to make a frame. To make your story picture sturdier, glue it to a piece of cardboard the same size.

Ndbele
Bead Bracelet

It's easy to make beautiful bracelets with wire and beads.

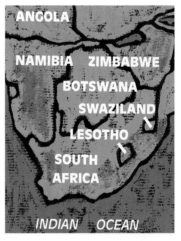

BEAD BRACELET

The Ndbele (en-duh-BAY-lay) people live in the Republic of South Africa and in Zimbabwe (zim-BAH-bway). Southern Ndbele women are known for making beautiful jewelry. They string tiny round glass beads together in rows on threads made from grasses.

In the past, Ndbele women wore bracelets and anklets every day. When they were young girls,

South Africa is located at the southernmost tip of the continent. Many European explorers arrived by sea more than 400 years ago. They brought beads and other craft materials to trade with the people of South Africa.

they began wearing beaded necklaces and bracelets around their neck and arms. They never took them off, and they added more beaded jewelry as they got older. For special events, Ndbele women often wore up to 50 pounds of jewelry!

Many Ndbele women no longer wear the heavy jewelry every day. But the skill of making beautiful designs with beads is still important to the Ndbele people.

This Ndbele woman and her child—standing in front of their painted house—wear traditional beaded clothing and jewelry.

HOW-TO PROJECT

This project shows you how to make a bracelet with colored beads. The Ndbele use small beads called seed beads. If you use medium-sized beads called pony beads, you can make a bracelet more quickly. Bags of pony beads are sold in bead stores, toy stores, and school supply stores.

You need:

Glass or plastic beads in red, white, and blue (or any 3 colors you like)
3 feet of thin wire
Needle-nose pliers or old scissors

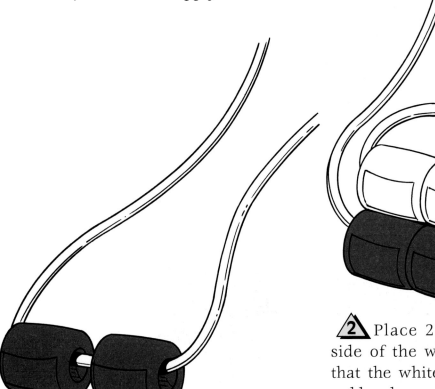

1 Cut a long piece of wire (about 3 feet). Place 2 red beads halfway down the wire.

2 Place 2 white beads on one side of the wire. Bend the wire so that the white beads lie next to the red beads.

Note: It's important to pull the wire very tight. Do not leave any loops at the end of each line of beads.

3 Push the other end of the wire through the white beads.

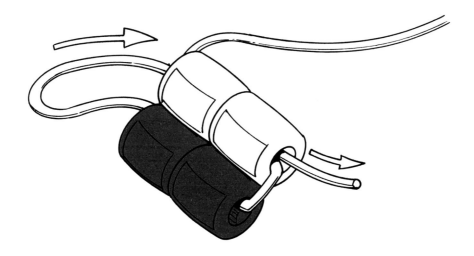

4 Repeat steps 2 and 3 with the blue beads. Continue adding lines of white, red, and blue beads.

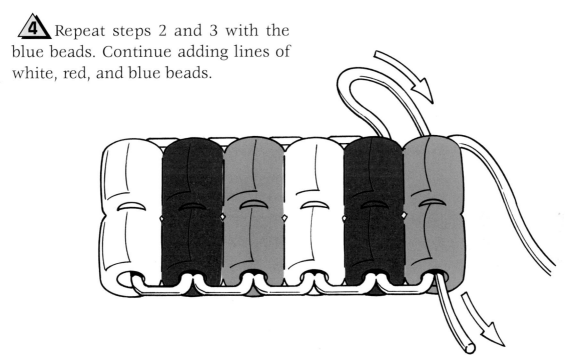

⑤ When the bracelet is long enough to reach around the widest part of your hand, it's ready to be finished. Push both ends of the wire through the first line of red beads, then through the next line of white beads. Cut the ends of the wire very close to the beads. If the ends stick out, they may scratch you.

Note: If the wire you are using is not long enough, you can make it longer by twisting on another piece of wire.

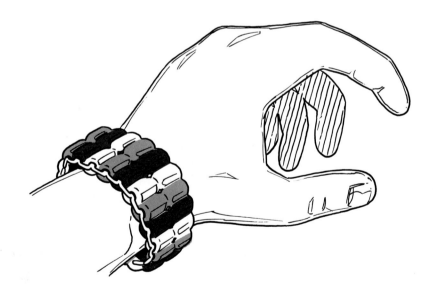

WHAT ELSE YOU CAN DO

Wider Bracelets: You can make wider bracelets by putting more than 2 beads in each row.

Other Patterns: Make up your own designs. By changing the colors in each row, you can make a pretty design.

Necklace: Cut a longer piece of wire and string it with many more beads.

Tutsi Basket

You can use your baskets to hold peanuts or other small snacks.

TUTSI BASKET

The earliest African baskets—including those made by the Tutsi (TOO-tsee) people—were made with the coiling method, which is still common. Long strands of dried grass are coiled around and around and bound together with thinner strands. Strands are added in end to end.

Tutsi girls learn basket weaving from their mothers, grandmothers, and aunts. They weave baskets of many kinds. Large storage baskets with lids hold

East central Africa is covered with cool mountains and high, flat land called plateaus (pla-TOHS). Many kinds of long grasses grow on the plateaus. These grasses are perfect for making baskets.

grain. The lids are pointed to help keep insects out. Some small baskets are woven together very tightly. Tutsi children can drink milk from these small baskets.

TECHNIQUE

Weaving is an old method still used for making baskets. Flat strands of grass are woven over and under each other to form the bottom and sides of a basket. Some strands can be dyed with leaves, bark, or fruit juices. By changing the number, color, and size of the strands, a basket maker can weave stripes, zigzags, and other designs into her baskets. Many shapes of basket are possible. Some baskets are open at the top. Others have handles or lids.

Take a close look at this basket. Can you tell where one strand ends and another one begins?

HOW-TO PROJECT

If you have access to long grasses or palm leaves, you can try to weave a basket just like Tutsi women do. But you can also make a basket from construction paper using the basic weaving technique. For a checkerboard pattern, use two different colors of paper. Glue will hold strips together neatly, but transparent tape is quicker.

You can keep jewelry, marbles, or scratch paper in your basket. Try using baskets instead of wrapping paper for small gifts. Or, at your next holiday or birthday party, put treats in baskets.

You need:

2 sheets of 9- by 12-inch red construction paper (or another color)
2 sheets of 9- by 12-inch beige construction paper (or another color)
Scissors
Compass or 5-inch plate and 9-inch plate
White glue and transparent tape
Pencil and ruler

1 Cut 8 strips of red construction paper. Each strip should measure 12 inches long and ¾ inch wide.

2 Glue the edges of 2 pieces of beige construction paper together. Cut 4 strips 16 inches long and ½ inch wide.

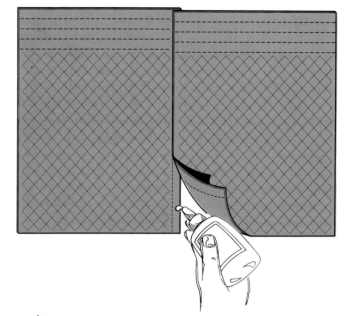

3 Glue 2 red strips in the middle to form a cross. Repeat this with the other red strips. You will have 4 red crosses.

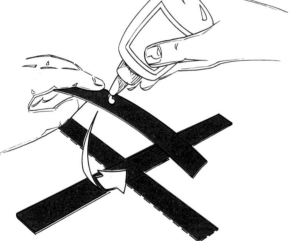

4 Place the 4 crosses on top of each other evenly. Glue them in place. They should look like a star.

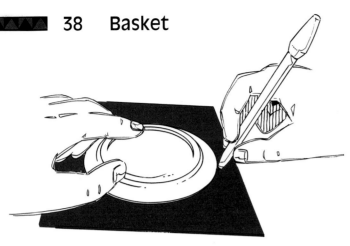

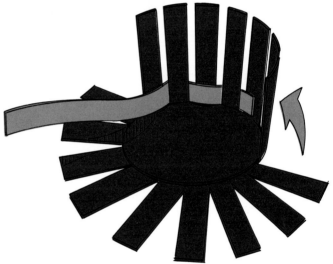

5 With a compass or plate, draw a circle 5 inches across on red construction paper. Cut out the circle and glue it to the center of the star.

6 Fold the rays of the star up around the edges of the circle. Tape a beige strip across the bottom of one ray. Weave it over and under the other rays all the way around. Remove the tape and glue the ends of the beige strip together. Hold the ends together until the glue begins to dry. Repeat with the 3 remaining beige strips.

7 Push the beige strips close to each other. Fold and glue the red ends to the inside of the basket, forming a rim.

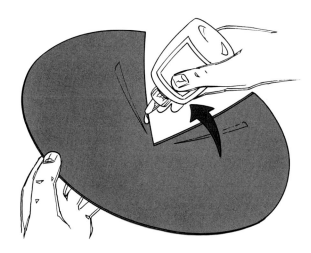

8 Make a pointed lid for the basket. Using a plate or a compass, draw and cut out a circle of beige construction paper 9 inches across. Cut a pie wedge (any size) out of the circle. Overlap and glue the cut ends together.

WHAT ELSE YOU CAN DO

Painting: Decorate your basket with tempera or acrylic paints.

Variations: You can change the size and shape of your basket using longer or wider strips of paper. Try making a basket from gift wrap or twisted paper rope (from craft stores).

Kigogo Game

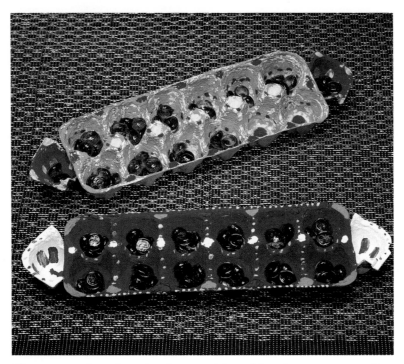

Kigogo can be played using marbles, dried beans, or small pebbles.

KIGOGO GAME

In Kenya, adults and children often relax by playing the game of kigogo (kee-GOH-goh). People play the game by moving seeds or other markers on a board that has 14 cups. Sometimes the game board is simply scratched into the ground. Two rows of six small holes are dug with another hole at each end of the rows. You can make a kigogo game from egg cartons, or you can dig one in the sand. Try this yourself the next time you are at the beach!

Many Kenyan people live and work in cities. But some families live in small towns and villages, where they work as farmers, fishers, and cattle herders.

In Kenya, kigogo boards are usually carved out of wood. Some Kenyan artisans carve their kigogo boards with animal figures and other designs. Kigogo is played in many parts of Africa. In different languages, the game is called *mankala, kigogo,* and *oware,* but it always means "transferring."

Left: This game board from Côte d'Ivoire uses polished seeds as markers.

Below: A game board from the Yoruba people of Nigeria

HOW-TO PROJECT

You can make your own kigogo game with empty egg cartons and peanuts, marbles, or dried beans. Follow the rules of the game as they are explained below. Although the rules are simple, the game is one of logic and skill. Planning your moves ahead of time increases your chance of winning.

> ### You need:
>
> 2 empty egg cartons, lids cut off
> 48 markers, which can be dried beans, peanuts, small pebbles, marbles, or small pieces of cardboard
> Transparent tape
> Scissors

1 Cut 2 egg cups from one of the egg cartons.

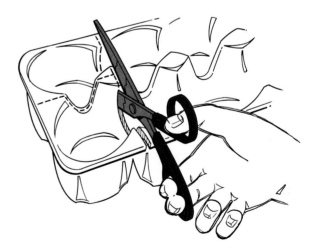

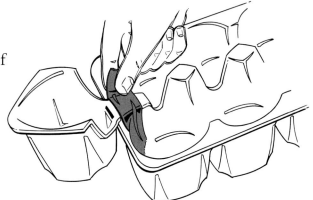

2 Attach 1 egg cup to each end of the other carton with tape.

3 To play the game, place the board between 2 players. Players own the 6 cups on the side nearest them and the end cup to the right. Players store any markers they win in this end cup. Put 4 markers in each of the middle 12 cups.

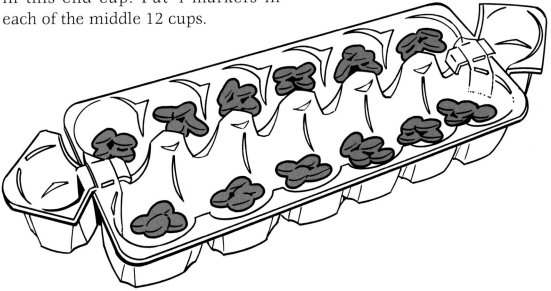

4 Always move the markers counterclockwise—in the opposite way a clock's hands move. The first player picks up 4 markers from any one of his or her cups. The player drops them, one at a time, into the cups, starting with the cup to the right of the emptied cup.

5 The other player then does the same thing, taking markers from the other side of the board. Players take turns, always taking all the markers in a cup and dropping them one by one in a line of cups. The number of markers in each cup will keep changing.

6 When a player drops the last marker in one of the other player's cups and that cup has either 2 or 3 markers in it, the player wins all of the markers in that cup. Players keep their winnings in the end cups on their right. The game is over when all the markers have been won. The winner is the player with the most markers in his or her end cup.

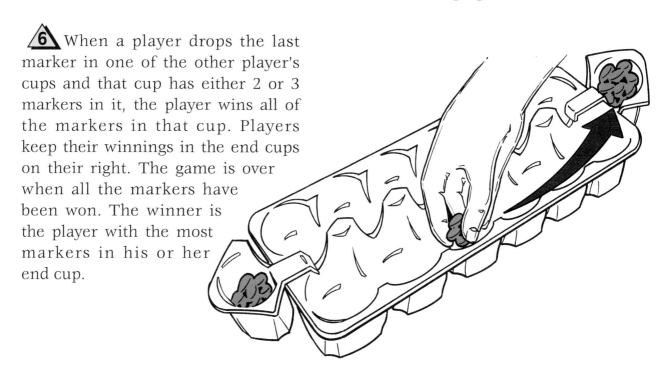

WHAT ELSE YOU CAN DO

Decorations: Paint your game board with tempera or poster paints. Cut letters, numbers, or special symbols from colored construction paper or felt. Glue the symbols to the sides of the egg cups.

Other Rules: In different parts of Africa, the game is played in different ways. After you have played kigogo a few times, you can invent your own rules. You can change the rules to make the game easier or more difficult. How about starting with 3 or 5 markers in each cup? How about agreeing that you can only win markers if there are 3 markers in 2 cups next to each other?

More Players: With 3 players, the third player uses an extra egg cup from the second egg carton. With 4 players, form teams of 2 players each.

Islamic Art Box

Any small box, such as a shoe box or a gift box, can be decorated with an Islamic pattern.

ISLAMIC ART

In the seventh century, Arab armies conquered the area of Africa known as Maghrib. They brought with them the Islamic religion. People who follow the Islamic faith are called Muslims. They believe that only Allah (God) creates living things. Because of this belief, Muslim artisans do not show humans

Morocco lies in the north-west corner of Africa, just across the Mediterranean Sea from Spain. Morocco was once part of a large African empire known as Maghrib—an Arabic word that means "the time or place of sunset."

or animals in their work. Instead, they create designs using geometric shapes such as squares and triangles. Islamic art also includes images of flowers, leaves, and Arabic script.

Woodworkers carve designs on walls, doors, furniture, and boxes. The patterns also appear on books, leather goods, brass trays, and ceramic tiles.

Tiles are often used to make mosaics (moh-ZAY-ix)—surfaces covered with repeated patterns of tile. Blue, turquoise, red, and gold are commonly used colors.

In Morocco, many buildings are completely covered with mosaics.

HOW-TO PROJECT

Here are two ways to decorate a box with an Islamic pattern. Both methods use tiles made from colored poster board.

You need:

Small cardboard or wooden box
   (such as a shoe or gift box)
Several sheets colored
   poster board
Ruler
2 or 3 felt-tip markers
Scissors
White glue

Design A

1 Cut poster board into 12 two-inch squares. Draw a line or a circle in one corner of each square.

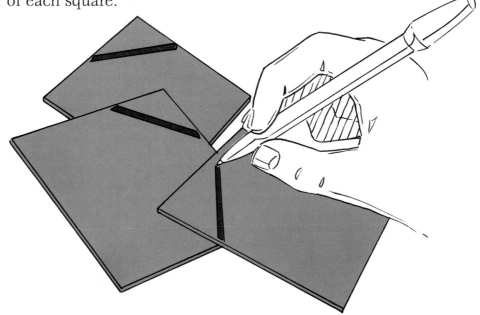

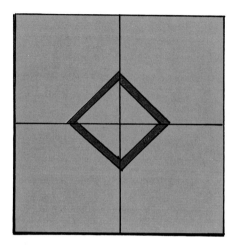

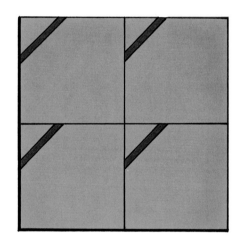

2 Arrange the squares into one of the patterns shown.

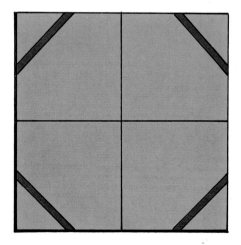

3 Glue the squares to the top of your box.

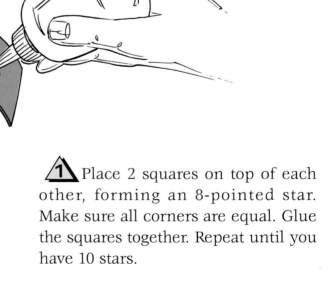

Design B

An 8-pointed star is often used in Islamic designs. Here is an easy way to make it.

1 Place 2 squares on top of each other, forming an 8-pointed star. Make sure all corners are equal. Glue the squares together. Repeat until you have 10 stars.

2 Glue the stars onto a box as shown. Do you notice that a cross pattern appears between the stars?

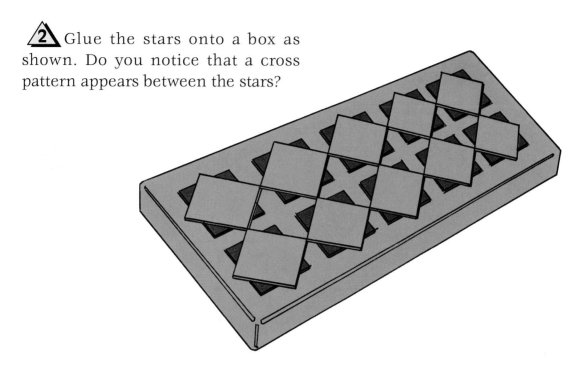

WHAT ELSE YOU CAN DO

Other materials: Cut your tiles from cardboard, then cover them with colorful wrapping paper.

T-shirts: Use scraps of fabric to make squares. Draw on the squares with permanent laundry markers or fabric paint. Glue or sew your design onto a T-shirt.

Guro Animal Mask

If you use your imagination, you can design many kinds of animal masks. A hippo, an antelope, and an elephant are just a few ideas.

ANIMAL MASKS

The Guro people create masks and costumes from wood and palm leaves. Masks with animal likenesses are worn by dancers at ceremonies to honor people who have died. Antelopes, elephants, hippopotami, hyenas, dogs, and monkeys are some of the animals represented.

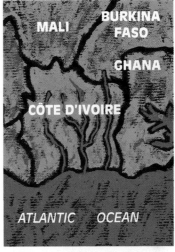

The Guro people live in the heart of Côte d'Ivoire. Wooded grasslands—called savannas—are home to many kinds of animals. Antelope, water buffalo, elephants, hippos, and monkeys can all be found there. Guro masks are often based on these animals.

Guro masks have both spiritual and entertainment value. The masks are worn by dancers and portray colorful faces. The most famous Guro dancers are often known by the names of their masks, rather than by their own names. People who watch the dancers clap and sing.

This Côte d'Ivorian mask is worn by a dancer.

HOW-TO PROJECT

In this project, you will create an elephant mask. Dried palm leaves are sometimes used when making elephant masks. Their wide tops and long, narrow bottoms suggest the shape of an elephant's head and trunk. You can make your elephant mask with poster board.

You need:

1 sheet white poster board, 22 inches by 28 inches
Acrylic paint or poster paint, several colors
2 feet of string
Ruler
Pencil
Scissors
Paper punch

1 Fold the poster board in half. Sharpen the crease by smoothing the folded edge with a ruler.

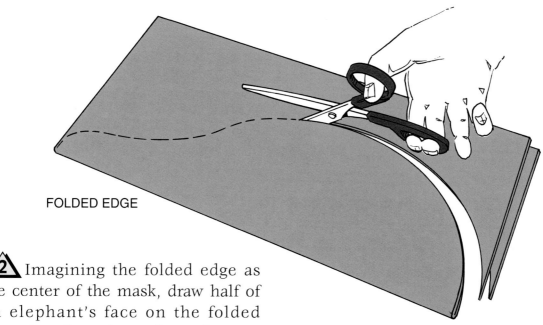

FOLDED EDGE

2 Imagining the folded edge as the center of the mask, draw half of an elephant's face on the folded edge. Cut along the outline. If it's too hard to cut through both layers, cut through one layer only. Then trace the other half of the mask on the other side of the poster board. Cut the mask out.

3 Draw features or designs on the mask with a pencil. Then decorate with paint.

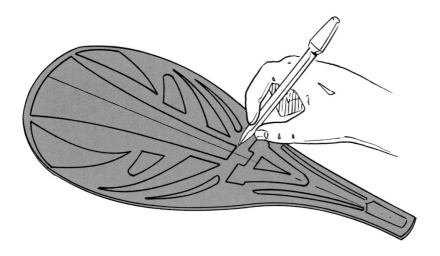

4 When the paint has dried, cut out the eyes. Punch a small hole on each side of the mask and tie 1 foot of string through each of the holes. Now you can wear your mask!

WHAT ELSE YOU CAN DO

Think of some other animals that would make fun masks. How would you make the horns of an antelope? Or the big snout of a hippopotamus? Or make a costume to go with your mask. Decorate an old sheet with paint or markers, cut a hole for your head, and wear the sheet like a poncho.

METRIC CONVERSION CHART

If you want to use the metric system, convert measurements using the chart on the right. Because fractions can be hard to work with, round all metric measurements to the nearest whole number.

when you know:	multiply by:	to find:
Length		
inches	25.00	millimeters
inches	2.54	centimeters
feet	30.00	centimeters
feet	.30	meters
yards	.91	meters
miles	1.61	kilometers
Volume		
teaspoons	5.00	milliliters
tablespoons	15.00	milliliters
fluid ounces	30.00	milliliters
cups	0.24	liters
pints	0.47	liters
quarts	0.95	liters
gallons	3.80	liters
Weight		
ounces	28.00	grams
pounds	0.45	kilograms

GLOSSARY

appliqué: A fabric cutout put on a larger piece of material for decoration

artisan: A person who is very skilled in making crafts

calabash: A kind of fruit. It grows on a vine, has a hard shell, and looks like a cucumber or squash.

chameleon: A small lizard that can change color and move its eyes in separate directions

culture: The customs, ideas, and traditions of a group of people. Culture includes religious celebrations, folktales, costumes, and food.

desert: A piece of land that cannot support most life because it is too hot and dry. Deserts often have a lot of sand and cacti.

ebony: A hard, black wood. Ebony is easy to carve, and it can be polished to a metal-like shine.

geometric style: A style of art that uses simple shapes, such as circles, triangles, and squares

iron ore: A rock or mineral that contains iron and is mined from the ground

mosaic: A picture or design made from small pieces of tile, wood, or other material

Muslim: A person who follows the Islamic religion. Muslims believe that Allah is the only god and that Muhammad is his prophet, or messenger.

papyrus: A water plant with tall stems. The people of ancient Egypt made the first paper from the papyrus plant's stems.

plain: A flat area of land that is usually covered with grass but has few or no trees

plateau: A large, flat piece of land that is raised above the surrounding land on one or more sides

rain forest: A large, woody land that gets at least 100 inches of rain every year. Rain forests are usually thick with plants, trees, and vines that block sunlight.

savanna: An area of land covered mainly with grasses, but also with scattered trees and shrubs

soapstone: A soft, white or gray rock that feels soapy or oily. It can be cut easily into shapes.

READ MORE ABOUT AFRICA

Fiction & Folktales

Dupré, Rick. *Agassu: Legend of the Leopard King.* Minneapolis: Carolrhoda Books, 1993.

Fairman, Tony. *Bury My Bones but Keep My Words: African Tales for Retelling.* New York: Henry Holt & Co., 1992.

Lewin, Hugh. *The Jafta Collection (series).* Minneapolis: Carolrhoda Books, 1983, 1984.

McDermott, Gerald. *Anansi the Spider: A Tale from the Ashanti.* New York: Holt, Rinehart, and Winston, 1972.

Mennen, Ingrid, and Niki Daly. *Somewhere in Africa.* New York: Dutton, 1992.

Steptoe, John. *Mufaro's Beautiful Daughters: An African Tale.* New York: Lothrop, Lee and Shepard, 1987.

Stock, Catherine. *Where Are You Going, Manyoni?* New York: Morrow Junior Books, 1993.

Tadjo, Veronique. *Lord of the Dance: An African Retelling.* New York: J.B. Lippincott, 1988.

Williams, Karen Lynn. *Galimoto.* New York: Lothrop, Lee and Shepard, 1990.

Nonfiction

Angelou, Maya. *My Painted House, My Friendly Chicken, and Me.* New York: C. Potter, 1994.

Griffin, Michael. *A Family in Kenya.* Minneapolis: Lerner Publications, 1987.

Haskins, Jim. *Count Your Way through Africa.* Minneapolis: Carolrhoda Books, 1989.

Kreikemeier, Gregory Scott. *Come with Me to Africa: A Photographic Journey.* Racine: Western Publishing Co., 1993.

McKenna, Nancy Durell. *A Zulu Family.* Minneapolis: Lerner Publications, 1986.

Musgrove, Margaret. *Ashanti to Zulu: African Traditions.* New York: Dial, 1976.

Onyefulu, Ifeoma. *A Is for Africa.* New York: Cobblehill Books, 1993.

Pitkänen, Matti A. with Reijo Harkonen. *The Children of Egypt.* Minneapolis: Carolrhoda Books, 1991.

INDEX

ABOUT THE AUTHOR

Florence Temko is an internationally known author of more than 30 books on world folkcrafts and paper arts. She has traveled in 31 countries, gaining much of her skill first-hand. Ms. Temko shows her enthusiasm for crafts through simple, inventive adaptations of traditional arts and crafts projects. She has presented hundreds of hands-on programs in schools and museums, including the Metropolitan Museum of Art in New York City and the Children's Museum in Boston. She lives in San Diego, California.

ACKNOWLEDGMENTS

The photographs in this book are reproduced through the courtesy of:

p. 6 (left), Turkish Republic, Ministry of Culture and Tourism; p. 6 (right), Wilford Archaeology Laboratory, University of Minnesota, by Kathy Raskob/IPS; p. 7 (left), Nelson-Atkins Museum, Kansas City, Missouri; p. 7 (right), Freer Gallery of Art, Smithsonian Institution; pp. 8, 9, 12, 18, 24, 28, 34, 40, 46, 52, Robert L. and Diane Wolfe; pp. 13, 35 © Frank L. Lambrecht, from the private collection of Dora Lambrecht; p. 19, Spink and Son Ltd., National Museum of African Art; p. 25, Eliot Elisofohn Photographic Archives, National Museum of African Art; p. 29 © South African Tourism Board; p. 41 (top) Jim Simondet; p. 41 (bottom) Franko Khoury, National Museum of African Art; p. 47 © Jason Laure; p. 53, Danyel Thibeault © ACDI/CIDA.

The maps and illustrations on pages 2, 11, 12, 13, 18, 19, 23, 24, 25, 28, 33, 34, 40, 46, 47, 52, and 57 are by John Erste.